Mary Violet

Aishwarya Mary George

BookLeaf
Publishing

Presentation by *BookLeaf Publishing*

Web: www.bookleafpub.com

E-mail: info@bookleafpub.com

ISBN: 9789357744744

First edition 2023

DEDICATION

To Thulasi, wouldn't have done this if it wasn't
for you

Symphony

On days that feel bled out of color
Flightless words die within
My breathless pin-pricked heart
Screams turn into whispers
Left behind are scars and blisters

Enveloped, it's soothing to drown
However a nudging tune lifts me out
I gasp for air, music fills my heart
I raise my chain, pointe and pirouette
Poised as a butterfly perched on a petal
Through half shut eyes,
I see a world coloured by dreams.

Silence (Haiku)

Wake up, the sun shines
To greet the rising souls
A silent battlefield

Deception (Epigram)

Over the past few days, I have been told thrice
Human relationships are built on an intricate set
of lies
Are these sayers so blind, have they not
realized?
That as architects, they are to be penalized.

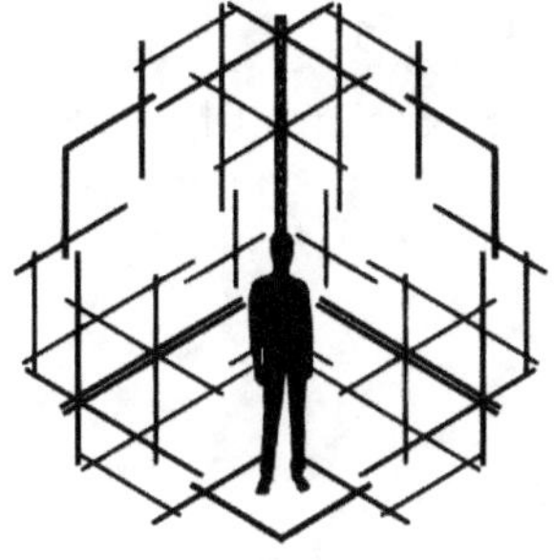

Hunger

A tangible, visceral yearning to be satisfied
Pesters us from birth to death, never defied
We hunger, we toil to fill a dimensionless void,
To steady shaky hands, or break apart the droid
All the while we take a measure of our pile
Of the mountain of this world's fruitful fountain
But minds feel led astray on foggy no man's
land
With a need to be reeled in, a purpose in hand
Little do we know, that the lost of us are
mistaken
To truly satiate, passion's fill needs to be taken.

Kikwit (Limerick)

There once was a man from Kikwit
He loved to pick for every event an outfit
For hours, he'd try on clothes
In front of the mirror, take exaggerated bows
Arrive a day late, and be kicked out of it.

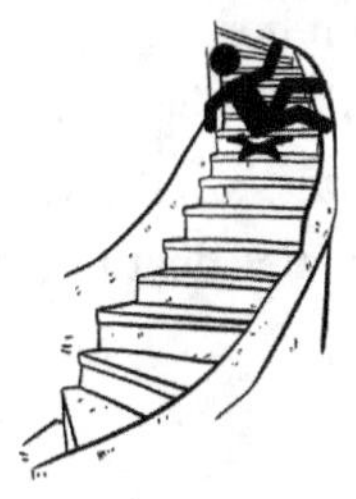

An elegy

Here lies she who was a mystery
For she was feared but also inspired
Here lies a true marker in history
Now in death, she's finally reconciled.

In awaiting her, millions found purpose
A muse to many, but treated a fiend
In her wake, soldiers painted a red canvas
But in her embrace they met their end.

What can we liken her to?
A field of white lilies blanketed by birdcries
Approaching winter, ornate with icicles few
Coldly calm, here lies death in its demise.

Ah la Figment

Have you met the folks of Ah La Figment
Well you must have, as they live in moments
Don't be confused, you will soon be enthused
Drawn in by the charm of their penchants

The first time I met them, they showed
When I took a quick bite of some rocky road
So in moments of ice cold numbness
Remember you might meet Mr. Fumbles

The next was when my hand shot out
Quick, to catch a falling glass, stout
In that moment of reflexive dash
Be sure to give my regards to Ms. Flash

Oh in Ah La Figment, I forgot to mention
There is one rule to gain admission
In your heart, you must be below eleven
Or in your mind, least believe in heaven.

To a friend?

The most mystifying in life are the subtle
differences
And none as confounding as loving vs being in
love
Ever so often my walled heart gets lost in
indulgences
Loving a lad, my friend, don't know why or how

Oddly boarded up gates once they are broken,
All restraint lost, a firm fumbling flood
flounders
When I miss him, every atom in me feels
awoken
When I lost him, wanting to be in love turned a
focus

How was I so foolish, when I have been here
before
There are multiple paths ahead, must I pick this
thorn?
Deceiving myself is an option, is it one to
explore?
Leading him on is an alternate, but my core I
would scorn

Lost I wander back, offering friendship as all I have
He says love is respecting, so we learn to stay ignorant
Moments pass, & at my foolish heart's desire I chaff
Why do I believe that this time it will be different?

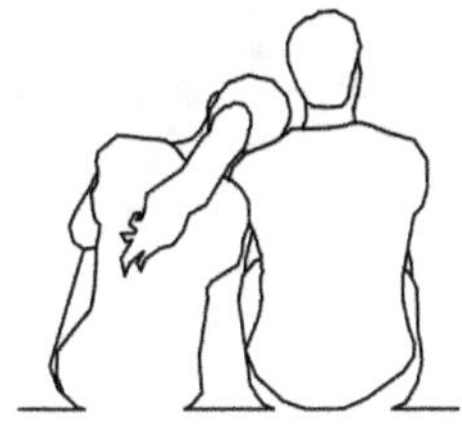

Silly (Limerick)

There was once a girl from Philly
Oh my, was she silly
She dreamed to fly like a kite
One day, jumped from a height
And landed on Mrs. Shrilly

Violet

At seven, when I learnt of heaven
I decided, If I were to be a color
I would be violet, I reckon

Black was the heavy weight
Of the cloud that uninvited settled
Smothering us at the hands of fate

Red was the fire that raged
When my dad shouted blind
As he raced to her side, uncaged

Blue were the tears that stained
Every cheek at the arctic funeral
Her youthful parting pained

White, the shade my face turned
As I realized I had lost her
Our journey together adjourned

In my mind, dawned a secret
Rather I would have to live for her
A life vibrantly hued like violet.

An epitaph

Here lies a fallen follicle
Well, now you are dead
Serves you right for being whimsical
You should have stayed on my head

Impermanence (Epigram)

Most decisions we don't make involve a
daunting fear
Of impermanence, what remains once the end
draws near?
Suffice to say, if we don't act, holding this dread
dear
We'll never know how it starts, lest which way it
will steer

Oxymoron

I have always wondered,
how I survived thus far
Now it's beginning to dawn,
It's because I'm an oxymoron

I led a life of disciplined chaos
However point most paramount,
I believed despite self scorn
In being a queen for all I had bourne

That explains the scars on my wrists
Not one of the fifty, ever fatal.

Busy

As the clock strikes two, I look up
No chairs rustle, no papers turn
Must have been a while with no one
A rat scurries past the barren floor
In the quiet, I had found nothing amiss
I began to ponder, why am I still here?
Am I running in this busy world,
In haste to catch up with it?
Or in disdain far away from it?
This answer I need, is this work theirs?
Or are these fruits of a passion mine?
With drooping heavy eyelids
I welcome sweet dreams.

A Walk in the dark

Walked around on a grassy path, that dark night
Out alone, ostensibly to figure out life
However the truth struck me, on return to
warmth
Just as a midnight walk loses its charm in the
light
Once deciphered, life ain't worth a fight.

Expectation

Often when queried on his sentiments
Over the years, towards his parents
He framed delicate resentment
Aided by their weighty expectation
Shouldered onto him at moments
Claiming him the worthy descendant

He was afraid of what the future held
If his actions, this animosity defined
So he hankered to rise above
To not let his path similarly entrap
A poor soul by expectation split
He chose the path lighted by love

Help

Plagued by an insane urge to pull back
Deeming seeking help a coward's act
But however isn't it an undeniable fact
That only the brave can seek solace
In the embrace of another's mind or heart

Plagued by an insane urge to push away
Deeming people, every problem's cause
But the truth remains, if they built the cross
From amongst their crowd, even Simon arose
This spells out the truth of the universe
Each other form the base of our live's traverse

Bliss

At the end of a winding day
I indulge in a childish play
All to help me unwind
Ignorant bliss I seek to find
And so I drown myself
And drown that day
In the sweet folds
Or the dark waves
Of Chocolate divine

History (Limerick)

The historian of ancient Politos
Was prone to making typos
She wrote, the emperor welcomed friends from
afar
Or was it welcomed fiends to a war
Ah now, she has rewritten history